What they said about the original e
American Child's Portfolio, The
Investing for Children.

"With education costs rising faster than inflation, parents cannot afford to wait to plan for their children's future. I highly recommend this book for any parent thinking about their children's future in the 21st century."

Brad Board, Principal
Deephaven elementary School

"I thoroughly enjoyed reviewing your wonderful book. I found it to be well written, honest and virtually error free."

P. Andrew Will
Manager, Consumer Deposit Products
Norwest Corporation

"I have never read such a practical, entertaining and caring book on investing."

Sis Tallman

"I have been in the investment business for 30 years. And to my knowledge, this is the first book to deal with a child's portfolio in a meaningful way."

Frank Hogan
Tax and Financial Consultant

"*An American Child's Portfolio* helped me to make a conscious and necessary decision to save money for my two daughters' future educational expenses. Dennis Paulaha's book helped me see how to do it without expensive help."

Kathi Bjorkman
Vice President
The Gaughan Companies

Little Tykoon

All you need to know about
saving and investing for children

D.F. Paulaha, Ph. D.

PATRON BOOKS

ISBN   978-0-9723619-6-5

First published 2010 by:
Patron Books
E-mail: patronbooks@sbcglobal.net

Contents

A Note to the Reader

When asked why they climb mountains, some say, "Because they are there."

Others say, "If you have to ask, you won't understand."

Both responses apply to this book.

There are mountains I hope we can help our children climb, just because they are there.

And if you have to ask why we should help our children climb those mountains, this book is probably not for you. This book is for everyone who does not have to ask the question.

Dennis Paulaha

Introduction

Button your shirt from the bottom up.

This is a book about how to save and invest for children.

It is based on a simple principle my father taught me when I was very young—a principle I have used every day of my life since then.

It was to button my shirt from the bottom up.

I believe that this "philosophy" applies to just about everything in life.

By starting at the bottom—getting the bottom straight before you begin—you can get almost anything right the first time.

You will almost never have to backtrack and start over.

And by the time you get to the more difficult stuff—the buttons at the top that are not so easy to see—it will be almost impossible to make a mistake.

Some of the ideas in this book were developed while I was researching and writing about economic and financial issues for the public. But the advice is practical and personal. It is, in large part a retelling of what I learned while determining what I could and could not do for my own young children.

D.F. Paulaha, Ph.D.

You Can Begin Today

The First Steps

IN THIS SECTION, you will see how to get started on a financial plan that can add thousands of dollars to your child's future.

You will not have to leave your house.

You will not have to call an outside expert.

And you can do it with money you might not think you have.

The first button: the shoebox portfolio

Begin with a shoebox.

Get a shoebox.

Then start filling it with money.

What money?

The loose change in your pocket or purse.

There is no better first step you can make in preparing a solid financial plan for your children.

Whether you are an expectant parent, a new parent, or the parent of a four, five, or ten year old, you can use a shoebox. But the sooner you begin, the better.

If you get started before your child is born, you will have a place to collect baby-shower money.

But no matter when you get started, whenever your child receives gift money, put it in the box.

And, whenever you can, throw in some, or all, of your spare change.

Then add the money that friends and relatives give your children. Instead of spending your child's gift money on cute little things, you will be saving it (and then investing it).

It might not seem like a lot of money at first. But it is worth much more than you might think.

Best of all, you will have set up a real financial plan.

And, once you have established your "shoe-box financial program," the "bigger" saving and investing decisions that come later will seem easy. They will simply be additions to what you already have.

Remember getting money when you were a child?

A small amount of money, by adult standards, was a big deal.

We all had a favorite aunt, uncle, or grandparent who slipped us a dollar at family gatherings, or who sent us five or ten dollars on our birthdays.

Whatever it was, it always seemed like a lot of money to a five or six year old.

What is the difference between "kid money" and "adult money?"

Partly, it has to do with what we buy. Kids can buy important things for less than a dollar. The things adults think are important often cost hundreds or thousands of dollars.

So it is easy to lose track of all the five- or ten-dollar gifts our children receive, which is why it is difficult for adults to think about using "kid money" to create a real portfolio.

But if you put birthday, holiday, and family-gathering money into your shoebox, before you know it, you will have easily saved $100 to $200, maybe much more.

The second button: turning "kid money" into "adult money"

Saving a child's gift money in a shoebox is pure common sense. Deciding what to do with the money as it accumulates has to make financial sense.

The main point is simple: If you do not have an easy way to save small amounts of cash, you can let thousands of dollars in future money slip through your fingers.

That is why the shoebox is so important.

It will help you secure thousands of dollars for your child's future.

It will also let you see how easy it is to put a financial plan into action.

Of course, a successful financial plan must also fit economic and tax conditions, not ignore them.

That is why it is important to understand the tax-advantaged accounts that exist today, as well as the investment markets; partly to understand the real options available, and partly so that you will not stay awake at night worrying about what you might be missing.

In other words, whatever you decide to do, you can do it knowing that the choices you make are based on knowledge and reason, not on "hot tips" or the constantly changing ideas and advice in magazine and newspaper columns.[1]

By now, you may be wondering if putting money in a shoebox a *real* financial plan?

I can guarantee you that it is. It is as real as anything an expensive consultant can dream up.

Of course, it is a limited plan.

Although it can provide thousands of dollars for your child's future, you will probably want to do more.

But doing more can be, and should be, just as simple and easy.

Without a simple and easy way to collect "small change," you can lose thousands of future dollars your children could have had.

And without a simple and easy way to deal with more "sophisticated" investments, I can guarantee you that bigger opportunities will disappear as well.

---

[1] Years ago, when I was writing investment newsletters, I tried to warn people of the fact that financial magazines, in order to be interesting to their readers, have to come up with new ideas every week or month. The problem is: Even if all their ideas are good, thoughtful, and sound, no one can start over every month or reorganize a portfolio every few days. As a result, magazines can make you crazy, or depressed, if you think about all the choices and all the things you did wrong—according to the latest issue.

You might still be thinking I am using a shoebox as an analogy, as a way to make a point about financial planning. I can promise you, I am not. I am absolutely serious when I tell you to get something you can use to collect small amounts of money.

Let me tell you why.

One of the major obstacles to saving and investing for our children is that the best time to make investments for children is when they are very young. Unfortunately, that is also the time when most of us can least afford to put much money away for our children.

The older our children get, and the older we get, the better we can afford to make investments for our children.

But the fact of life about investments is that they appreciate in value over time!

Therefore, the more time they have to earn interest or appreciate in value, the more they will be worth.

As a result, your "shoebox portfolio" can be the equal of thousands of dollars transferred to children when they reach their teens.

So there is a practical reason for doing as much as you can when your children are very young.

And one thing we can all do is make certain that the money our young children receive does not slip away.

Besides, the principles behind our simple beginning and the principles behind more "sophisticated" plans are the same:

Save money in an easy-to-deal-with place.

As the money accumulates, invest it or transfer it to an account where it will earn interest or can be used to purchase appreciating assets.

In what follows, you will see how to prepare bigger plans.

But, if you get a shoebox, you will have made the right start. You will be buttoning your shirt from the bottom up.[2]

---

[2] If it were possible, I would require everyone reading this book to put the book down now, find a shoebox, and put the loose change in his or her pocket or purse in the shoebox before going on to the next chapter.

A "Bigger Shoebox"

NOW THAT YOU have taken the first steps toward securing your child's financial future, the next question is: What do you do with your shoebox money?

Of course, the answer to that question begins with another question, which is: Can your child's portfolio be held in a way that yields tax-free earnings?

The answer is: Yes, it is possible to invest money in ways that avoid taxes.

And because, for most of us, there is no reason to pass up the tax savings, what you do with your shoebox money will be affected by the tax advantages available.

1. A Coverdell Education Savings Account

OKAY. Where should you put your shoebox money?

If your child is a newborn or not yet in school, one of the best places to put your shoebox money is in a Coverdell Education Savings Account.

There are many reasons for putting the money in a Coverdell ESA account:

The earnings (interest or appreciation) on investments grow tax-free.

Withdrawals used for eligible education expenses are tax-free.

And you can invest the money in the account any way you choose.

You can open a Coverdell education savings account with your bank or broker; and the account, which is often described as a "type" of IRA account, can be in your child's name or your name with your child as the beneficiary.

However, unlike some "real" IRA accounts, the contributions are not tax deductible.

Although the contributions must be in cash (you cannot transfer stock you already own into a Coverdell account), once the money is in the account, you can invest the funds in bonds, mutual funds, individual stocks, money market vehicles, and so on.

Another bonus is that any adult can make contributions to the account, whether or not he or she is a relative, which means it is a great way for friends, relatives, and godparents to give money to young children.[3]

---

[3] In fact, contributions can even be made by a child to his or her own account.

There are, however, two restrictions.

One is that the annual contributions—from all contributors—cannot be more than $2,000 a year for each child. If you exceed the limit, there is a 6 percent penalty.

The second is that there is an income limit of $95,000 for a single parent and $190,000 for parents who are married and file a joint return. If your income exceeds the limit, there is a declining scale of allowable contributions that eventually reaches zero. If your adjusted gross income is above the top limit ($110,000 for individuals and $220,000 for a joint return), you cannot make any contributions to a Coverdell ESA without paying a penalty.

As long as you meet the contribution limit, you can add funds up to the April 15th tax-filing deadline of the next year. And you can have as many Coverdell ESAs as you want, although the $2,000 limit applies to the total contributions to all Coverdell accounts for each child.[4]

---

[4] Some people open one account at a bank and a second account with a broker.

There is one other potential disadvantage of a Coverdell ESA. The funds must be used for qualified education expenses by the time the beneficiary is 30. If your child decides to not use the funds for college, he or she must, within 30 days after his or her 30th birthday, withdraw all the money and declare the earnings as taxable income, plus pay a 10 percent penalty.

As bad as that might sound, it is a disadvantage that could turn out to be a future advantage, because the tax and the penalty can be avoided if the entire account is transferred to another Coverdell ESA for another family member, which could be your child's own son or daughter.

As such, if your child decides not to go to college, or if he or she receives a scholarship, so that the Coverdell money is not needed, the funds can be transferred to his or her child (or children). That means your grandchild will begin life with a substantial account that will continue to grow tax-free. And it reduces the contributions your son or daughter will make to his or her child's future.[5]

Another advantage, which will not affect many people, is that the funds can be used for K-12 expenses.

The most important restriction, of course, is the $2,000 annual contribution limit. Which is why you may want to create a second account.

Which brings us to the next step.

---

[5] There is a lot of information about Coverdell accounts on the Internet.

2. The 529 College Savings Program

IF YOU ARE ABLE TO contribute more than $2,000 a year to your child's account when he or she is very young, you can add a 529 college savings program to your child's education portfolio.[6]

The 529 program is a tax-advantaged program based on IRS code 529 (hence, the name) that is administered by individual states, each of which contracts with a commercial bank to manage the funds.[7] Because the program is normally overseen by each state's department of education, there is a good chance you will receive some information when your child begins school. But you can create an account before then.

When you open a 529 account (often called an EdVest plan), your child is listed as the designated beneficiary and your contributions are placed in a trust fund established by the state. You then choose a specific investment program from a number of options offered by the fund's manager. It may be a stock portfolio, a bond portfolio, or a portfolio made up of a combination of investment categories.

You cannot, however, manage the funds in a 529 account yourself, which means you cannot choose to invest your funds in a specific stock. Which is why there can be a legitimate reason to have a Coverdell account in addition to a 529 plan. Which is why I like the idea of setting up a Coverdell account, rather than a 529 plan, when your child is born, or very young, even though most parents will add a 529 plan.

---

[6]To go along with your Coverdell account.

[7]In Wisconsin, for example, EdVest is administered by the Wisconsin Office of the State Treasurer and is managed by Wells Fargo Funds Management, LLC.

The interest earnings and asset appreciation in a 529 plan, as well as qualified withdrawals, are free from federal and state taxes. And although all states allow contributions to be made by parents, grandparents, great-grandparents, aunts, or uncles, the contributions are deductable for state tax purposes only for the person who lists the child as a deduction;[8] and in no case are the contributions deductable for federal taxes.

You can use the funds to pay for education expenses at any eligible school—including two-year and four-year colleges, technical, vocational, and graduate schools—even if the school is not in your home state.[9] And when you withdraw the funds, they are free of federal and (normally) state taxes if used for qualified educational expenses.

You can set up an automatic investment plan or a direct payroll deposit of as little as $15 a month.

You have to make an initial contribution (normally about $250) to open an account. (A good thing to do with your shoebox money, although the initial contribution is often waived if you set up your account with an automatic contribution plan.)

You can contribute up to $330,000 in total (depending on the state) for each child (more than virtually anyone should put in an education fund).

And contributions can be made by check, electronic funds transfer, Federal Wire, automatic investment, and payroll deduction.

---

[8] In Wisconsin contributions up to $3,000 per year, are deductable from state taxes for each contributor.

[9] Qualified expenses include tuition, fees, books, room and board.

So, now you have a Coverdell account that lets you make specific investments with contributions up to $2,000 a year (of course, it is not necessary to make the maximum contribution) and a 529 plan that lets you set up automatic deposits with virtually unlimited contributions. What are you missing?

As we will see, nothing that matters.

3. Roth IRAs

MANY ADVISORS recommend that you use a Roth IRA as a place to save for college.

From a tax-saving standpoint, a Roth IRA is about the same as a Coverdell account or a 529 (EdVest) Plan.

Contributions are not tax deductible.

But earnings are tax free if the funds are used for education.

And you choose how your contributions are invested.

As such, a Roth IRA can be a great way to save and invest for college.

In fact, for some, it can be a better alternative than either a Coverdell ESA or a 529 plan. You can open a Roth IRA when you child is born (or before), and make after-tax contributions that grow tax-free.

Although the Roth IRA was designed as a retirement fund, the law specifically says that withdrawals used for higher education expenses are not subject to taxation.

My only concern is that, because a Roth IRA is a great way to save for your own retirement, you may not want to use it as an education account, because the alternative plans are just as easy and just as tax-free.

Of course, Congress is constantly fiddling with the laws governing all of these plans.

The maximum contribution to Coverdell accounts was lowered from $2,000 per year to $500 per year and then raised again to $2,000; and you can use Coverdell money for K-12 expenses.[10]

Contributions to a Roth IRA are also limited by your adjusted gross income. The maximum annual contribution is $5,000 per year ($6,000 if you are over 50); but as your income increases past a stated level, the maximum allowable contribution decreases. Current limits are $105,000 for an individual and $166,000 for a joint return. Of course, even if you meet the income limits, there is the $5,000 (or $6,000) limit for annual contributions. Which means that if you set up a Roth IRA with the idea that you can use some of the funds for education, there may not be much left for you.

The 529 education saving plan allows much larger annual after-tax contributions, and the same tax savings as the Roth IRA

That is why most parents will come out ahead by having a Coverdell account and/or a 529 plan for their children, and a Roth IRA for themselves.

---

[10] For a while, Congress seemed intent on legislating the Coverdell account out of existence. Then there was a reversal that brought back the benefits.

Shoeboxes You Don't Need

YOU WILL MOST LIKELY HEAR OR READ about a lot of ways to save and invest for children.

My belief is that if something exists in the financial world, it must be good for someone; otherwise it would not exist.

Two examples are custodial accounts and trust funds. Each exists because it offers benefits for particular individuals or families.

But, and this is what matters, neither has anything to offer most families.

1. Custodial Accounts

A CUSTODIAL ACCOUNT lets an adult make individual investments in a child's name.

But the only reason for making investments in a child's name is to gain a tax advantage. And you can do that better with a Coverdell ESA and/or a 529 plan—and with less risk.

In the distant past, parents could gain a tax advantage by transferring funds into a child's account, making investments that were taxed at the child's lower rate, then switching the money back into their name.

In other words, it was never the child's money. Eventually, Congress decided that people—especially wealthy parents—were taking advantage of a loophole in the tax law; and in 1986 a new tax law was passed.

The 1986 law changed two things:

1) Tax rates on children's accounts were increased.

2) All transfers or gifts made to either a custodial account or a trust fund were made irrevocable—which means once the money is transferred to the child's account, it is the child's money. Period. Parents cannot take the money back without paying a stiff penalty.

As a result, custodial accounts now offer both smaller advantages and greater dangers.

Today, the main reason for understanding the basics of custodial accounts and trust funds is so that you will know you are not missing out on anything.

To begin with, a custodial account is exactly what it sounds like.

It is an account in your child's name with you or another adult named as custodian.

You can open a custodial account at a brokerage firm, bank, or mutual fund.

All you need is a Social Security number for your child and a few minutes to take care of the paperwork.

The advantages of custodial accounts are:

* It is an easy place to deposit money on a regular or irregular basis.

* The investments are in the child's name, which means there is a small tax advantage if your child is fourteen or older.

* Any money deposited will automatically earn competitive short-term interest rates.

* It is easy to switch from interest-bearing assets to other assets, such as stocks, bonds, etc.

* If someone other than you is listed as the custodian, the funds in the account are not considered to be part of your estate, which means the funds can avoid probate. In most cases, that is a marginal advantage, and it is recommended that you and your spouse be listed as joint custodians.

* There are normally no fees for such accounts.

The disadvantages are:

* The tax break for children under fourteen years of age is small.

* All the money put into such accounts is an "irrevocable" gift to the child.

* The earnings are NOT tax-free. Earnings are taxed at the child's rate (which is not normally zero).

For most families, the disadvantages of custodial accounts outweigh the advantages. Most important is that you cannot give money to a child by putting it in a custodial account and then take the money back later. If you do, you will pay a large penalty. For most of us, once we give money to our children, we are not going to take it back anyway.

But there are two things to consider.

One is that, because of unforeseen circumstance, you might need the money more than your children do at some time in the future.

The other is that as soon as your child reaches the "age of majority" (18 to 21 years old, depending upon your state law), he or she can bring a birth certificate to your broker or banker and withdraw all the funds.

Looking at a three-month old baby asleep in a crib, the last thing you would worry about is that he or she might "squander" your savings. But if you look at 16- or 17-year olds, you may decide that you have a reason to be cautious.

There is a tax advantage to letting funds accumulate in a child's name in a custodial account—mainly after the child turns fourteen. But the savings come at a cost: You cannot maintain control of the money, as you can with a Coverdell Account, a 529 Plan, or even a Roth IRA. And you still pay taxes!

Trust funds

If you live in a state where your child does not reach the age of majority until 21, it is possible that you will spend all, or most, of the funds in a custodial account on college expenses before the child takes control.

An alternative idea is to set up a trust fund.

Unfortunately:

* Trust funds are more complicated than custodial accounts.

* Unlike trust funds of the past, today's do not offer any great tax advantages.

* Trust funds can be expensive to establish.

* Like a custodial account, trust funds require an irrevocable gift—once the funds are put into a trust fund, they belong to the child.

The main advantage of a trust fund is that it can give you more control over how the funds are used. By paying an attorney to set up a trust fund, you can specify how and when the assets will be distributed to the child. But the attorney's fee can be $1,500, or more, depending upon how detailed you want to get.

There are no "rules" for trust funds. Each is a separate and unique legal entity. Which is why they can be expensive to set up.

And if you have a bank act as trustee, the bank will most likely charge you an annual fee plus a percentage of the account's total value. It is common for a bank to charge $500 per year plus one percent of the fund's value.

Taxes on Custodial Accounts and Trust Funds

Because of the different tax schedules for custodial accounts and trust funds, a trust is better than a custodial account only if it has a value of more than $50,000 or $60,000. But the tax savings must be weighed against the cost of setting up and administering a trust.

If you are able to manage a trust yourself, with no expenses, the trust may come out ahead.

If you do decide to set up a trust, the simplest and least expensive is a "minor's trust." If you find the right attorney, the initial cost could be only a few hundred dollars. But you will still have additional tax forms to deal with each year; the tax savings are not what you might have expected; and the money still belongs to the child, although most of it may be spent during college, before the fund is turned over to the child at age 21 (which is the case with a "minor's trust").

Of course, the main reason for custodial accounts and trust funds is to reduce taxes.

But the key word is "reduce," because custodial accounts and trust funds *reduce* taxes—they do not eliminate taxes.

Therefore, if you are going to make an irrevocable gift to your children by creating a custodial account or a trust fund, thereby giving up eventual control of the money, or having to pay an attorney to maintain some control, what are you or your children getting in return? Not much. A small saving on taxes if you invest outside a Coverdell account or a 529 plan—because some of the earnings are taxed at the child's rate, rather than yours. That's all.

On the other hand, if you use a Coverdell, 529, or Roth IRA plan, you avoid all taxes on all earnings.

6. On Your Own—Ignoring the Tax Breaks

There are five tax-avoidance opportunities:

Three avoid all taxes on earnings:
* Coverdell Education Savings Accounts.
* 529 College Savings Programs (EdVest accounts).
* Roth IRAs.

Two can reduce taxes on earnings
* Custodial accounts.
* Trust funds.

A sixth option is to save and invest on your own, ignoring some, but not all, tax breaks.

For some parents, the tax savings might not seem worth taking the time, effort, and money to set up a tax-avoidance plan. That is your decision.

Comparing Coverdell and 529 Plans

IF YOU WANT TO TAKE ADVANTAGE of the tax breaks offered by a Coverdell account or a 529 plan or both, there are some differences you should be aware of.

1. Things to know

You can have both a Coverdell ESA and a 529 plan for a child.

Neither offers tax deductable contributions.

Each offers tax-free interest accumulation and asset appreciation.

Each offers tax-free withdrawal of funds for qualified education expenses.

Qualified education expenses for Coverdell ESAs include primary and secondary school.

Qualified education expenses for 529 plans must be for higher education.

Coverdell ESAs have a lower annual contribution limit ($2,000 versus $13,000 or more per year for a 529 plan).

Coverdell ESAs let you choose specific investments; 529 accounts limit your choices to portfolio "bundles" offered by the fund's manager.

Coverdell ESAs must be used for education before the beneficiary turns 30, and contributions to the account must stop when the beneficiary turns 18.

There are no age limits for a 529 plan. Contributions can be made at any age and the funds can be used at any age, which means they can pay for graduate school or for an adult returning to school.

If you have a 529 plan and your child receives a college scholarship, you can withdraw funds from the account equal to the value of the scholarship, without paying taxes or a penalty.

If you have a Coverdell ESA and your child receives a college scholarship, you will have to transfer the unused funds to another family member; or pay taxes and a penalty on the withdrawal.

When applying for financial aid at a college, the funds accumulated in either a Coverdell ESA or a 529 plan will not be included in your child's financial portfolio.

If your child decides not to attend college, both 529 and Coverdell accounts can be switched to another family member, with no penalty for switching and without paying taxes if the funds are eventually used to pay for the new person's education (which, for a 529 account, could even be you or your spouse).

The beneficiary listed in either a Coverdell ESA or a 529 plan can be changed at any time.

Funds in a Coverdell ESA can be moved to a 529 plan.

For a Coverdell ESA, if the beneficiary does not use the funds for education before he or she turns 30, the money must be withdrawn within six months of his or her 30th birthday and taxes paid on the earnings, along with a penalty (as much as ten percent).

The Coverdell age issue can be avoided by transferring funds from one Coverdell account to another Coverdell account set up for a family member of the original beneficiary or to a 529 fund, a switch that might be necessary if your child decides against college. In either case, the funds will then be available to another family member without the Coverdell's age restriction that requires that they be spent by the time the original beneficiary reaches the age of 30.

Summary

Although we have not yet discussed the details of individual investments, you already have a complete, stand-alone financial program.

If you do nothing more than what we have already discussed, you will have a solid financial plan for your child:

* Get a shoebox to save the gift-money your child receives.
* Add some of your loose change whenever you can.
* Periodically transfer the cash to one or more tax-advantaged accounts, or to your own investment accounts.
* Use automatic or periodic contributions to add more funds to the account(s).

I hope you will read on.

I hope you want to do more.

But, if you limit your plans to what has already been discussed, your children will already be assured a better start in life.

Three Principles of Success

BEFORE WE GO ON, I want to discuss three important investment principles:

1) Keep it simple.
2) Relax.
3) Take control.

Using our shirt-buttoning analogy one more time, these three principles represent buttoning the next three buttons.

Although these principles may seem obvious, they are easy to forget; and if you forget the basics, your plans can go astray before you know what happened.

Many people believe that financial plans are cut-and-dried, follow-the-rules kinds of activities. They are not. Financial plans are as much a way of thinking as a way of acting. If that were not true, everyone would be equally successful, which is not the case.

To be successful, you have to follow the basic principles of success.

1. Keep it simple

There was a time, not too long ago, when the only telephones we had were in our home or office. When the phone rang, it was up to us to answer it or not. We had complete control, especially when they invented Caller ID, because the caller could not know if we were home or not. And when we left our home or office, there was a chance for a little peace, because no one could call us and we could not call anyone (unless we used a pay phone).

Those days are gone. Now everyone above the age of ten has his or her own cell phone, a product that some might see as the greatest invention since the wheel. Cell phones *are* great; they let us be in contact with everyone all the time. Of course, they also let everyone be in contact with us *all the time*. So, along with the advantages of cell phones, there are some real disadvantages. The most important is that we have less control of our time, because it is virtually impossible to not answer incoming calls and because we are under constant pressure to make outgoing calls. No matter where we are, our friends and business contacts know we can (and should!) call them from everywhere, even when we are on vacation.

Because of cell phones, we can never be alone. Even if we do not answer a cell phone, it is right there, ringing away. And we know we will need an excuse for not answering. Or for not quickly returning a call.

Although we do not want to turn back progress, we can still appreciate the plain old telephone. It was a marvel. It did exactly what we wanted it to do. It let us communicate easily with others. It was simple. It was easy to use. We could do other things while we were talking. It got the job done. And we could walk away from it when we left the office or home to do other things. Of course, we missed some calls.

But, by making the product *better, more advanced,* we also destroyed some of its benefits.

Financial plans are the same. Some are simple and basic and get the job done. Others demand more of our time and energy.

The basic purpose of saving and investing for our children is to give them a better chance for a successful and happy life.

Keep it simple; it works. Complicate it—by devising a plan that is too demanding—and it may be doomed. It can take over your life, without providing anything more than can be achieved with a simple plan. And the children lose.

Much of what is written about saving and investing, either for adults or children, sounds exciting. It sounds fantastically easy and profitable. It can sound like the greatest idea since the wheel.

In practice, the pie-in-the-sky benefits are often overshadowed by extra costs, extra demands on your time and energy, and greater risks.

You do not need a financial plan for your children that is the equivalent of a cell-phone. You need a plan you can implement and follow, not a plan that follows you around wherever you go, ringing in your ears.

What most of us need is a basic plan, something like old-time, basic, landline telephone service.

If you have such a plan, you are almost assured of making your life and the lives of your children better.

2. Relax

A few years ago, a financial writer published a book of ideas for financing a college education.

One of the ideas was to purchase a rental house near the college your child attends. Instead of paying for a dormitory or apartment, your child lives in the house. To help pay for the mortgage, your child rents out rooms to other students. And when your son or daughter graduates, the house is sold for a profit that recovers part of his or her tuition and book expenses.

Sounds good. I am sure the plan could work. I am sure it did work. But if you are not already a real-estate investor, you may not want to manage property halfway across the country.

Besides, if your children are going to be landlords and maintenance people while they are in college:

What will happen to their grades?

What will happen during vacations?

Who will be responsible for the property during the summer?

Plus: Real-estate profits are far from guaranteed, especially if you are going to hold the property for only four or five years. Rents might not cover the mortgage. And any house can lose value.

In the end, you could end up with real-estate losses on top of college costs, while also disrupting your children's lives and grades.

Such schemes can also stab your other plans in the back. By assuming that you have college expenses all "figured out," you may decide it is OK to drop your real financial plans. In effect, you could end up betting your child's future on a financial scheme you may not be able to put into practice when the time comes.

The "buy-a-rental-house" scheme is simply a real estate investment plan. If you believe that real estate is a good investment, do it yourself—now. Don't wait until your children are in college to buy a house for them to manage. Buy one now, and manage it yourself, with the idea that the profits will be used to finance a future college education. But don't mix everything together.

More importantly: Relax. Stick with simple ideas that make sense to you. Have fun with what you are doing.

Over the years, you will run into hundreds of investment schemes for your children.

Each time, ask yourself the following four questions:

1) Will it take time I don't have?

2) Is it something I can actually do?

3) Is there a risk of losing all or part of my investment, including the time it demands?

4) Will it take funds away from my basic investment plan?

Most of the ideas you will read about are specialized plans for people with special skills, knowledge, and circumstances. Few have anything to offer a real family.

It would be nice if we could all take advantage of every clever idea. But that will not happen.

So, instead of creating a cell-phone financial plan, it is better to think about a plan that you can control.

If you relax and stick to a plan that fits your own family's circumstances and needs, you will be more successful and happier.

3. Take control

A friend of mine—also an economist—thought it might be fun, and profitable, to be a stockbroker for a while. After teaching for ten years, he wanted a break from the academic life. He thought he knew a lot about what stockbrokers are supposed to know. He also thought he knew something about dealing with people. After all, students are people.

He saw an ad from a national brokerage company in the local paper. They were looking for stockbrokers. So he called.

He expected them to be impressed by his Ph.D. and all his years of teaching experience. He was certain he would be a successful broker. He was certain he was one of the most qualified candidates ever to respond to one of their ads.

What more could they possibly want?

They wanted a good vacuum-cleaner salesman.

That's what the sales manager told him.

The sales manager was so certain that my friend's economic training would be a detriment rather that an asset, that my friend could not even get an interview.

Why a vacuum-cleaner salesman instead of a trained economist? Because a stockbroker is a salesperson. His or her job is to sell you investments that will, hopefully, meet "your" needs.

The fact is: We buy most of our investments from salespeople.

If you want straightforward, personal investment advice and counseling, you are going to have to pay for it.

But if you are like most of us, you are going to get a lot of advice and counseling from people who earn their livings by selling you something.

There is nothing wrong with salespeople. They help us buy what we want, from our homes, cars, clothing, computers, vacuum cleaners, and television sets, to our investments in stocks, bonds, real estate, precious metals, and fine art.

The best salespeople take their jobs very seriously.

In fact, a good salesperson can be more knowledgeable than a not-so-dedicated consultant. Some of the most successful salespeople actually *sell knowledge.* They do the work we do not have time for and give us legitimate choices to make—choices that can help us meet our own individual objectives.

But—and this is what is important—you can run into big trouble if you forget that salespeople are salespeople and assume that they can do more than they can do.

I do not want to imply that salespeople cannot be trusted. That is not true. But I do want to state as clearly as possible that they should not be trusted to provide advice and knowledge they cannot be expected to have, especially when that advice is crucial to our children's future.

As a rule, the salespeople you work with have your best interests in mind. They earn a living by selling investments to steady clients. And to keep steady clients happy, salespeople have to try their best.

The point of the vacuum-cleaner salesman story is not to make you suspicious of brokers. It is to help you see that you must accept the responsibility of guiding your own plan.

Many, maybe most, of your investments will be purchased from stock brokers or commercial banks.

If you are clear about your objectives and about the risk you are willing to accept, you can get a lot of help from brokers. They have access to more information and investment products than you will ever need.

But you should not hand control over to your broker. Not because your broker cannot be trusted, but because your broker cannot be expected to have either the training or the time to be your own personal financial planner and manager.

That is your job.

Summary of a basic financial plan

As simple as it might sound, if you follow the advice above, you will have a real financial plan in place.

* You will have decided to save money for your child.
* You will have an easy and accessible place to save "loose" money—a shoebox, paper bag, or whatever.
* You will have something to do with the money as it accumulates: Put it in a tax-advantaged account, such as a Coverdell ESA, a 529 (EdVest) savings plan, or both.
* You can contribute up to $2,000 a year to a Coverdell ESA you open with your bank or brokerage firm so that you can make individual investment choices yourself. (A Coverdell ESA is a great way to get started when your child is very young; and if the potential disadvantages are upsetting, they can be avoided by switching the funds to a 529 plan later.)
* You will set up periodic contributions (virtually unlimited with a 529 savings plan).
* You will have decided to keep it simple—to concentrate on a straightforward plan. No cell-phone financial programs.
* You will have decided to relax—to not to let all sorts of investment schemes sidetrack your simple, basic plan.
* You will have recognized that you—not a salesperson— must be the ultimate manager; that you must be in control.
* You will have guaranteed your children a better financial future.
* You will have accomplished more than the vast majority of parents in America.

One final note: If you are relatively wealthy, you may be thinking that a shoebox investment plan is not for you.

That may be true.

But I want you to think about an important fact. The wealthier you are, the more "loose money" is going to come your child's way. For example, your child will probably receive more and larger cash gifts than many other children. Therefore, the future value of the money you may spend without thinking will be considerably greater as well.

In a few pages, we will examine a large number of investment opportunities.

But, before looking at your investment options, I want to discuss need.

Need

We all have goals or objectives.

And we all make assumptions about what is needed to reach those goals.

One of our most important goals is to help our children have the best life possible.

The question is: What do we need to make that come true?

One thing most parents need is this book.

That probably sounds a little self-serving, and I suppose it is. But while I was reviewing my research files, I kept thinking, "There is so much information out there, no one needs this book. Anyone who wants to put in the time can read countless articles and books telling them what to do. Add in the Internet and the radio, and there is more than anyone can read. Plus, most of what is available makes sense. Therefore, there really isn't anything I can say that hasn't already been said by someone else."

Then I realized that the more information there is on a subject, the greater is the need to know how to separate the good from the bad; and to have a foundation that can be used to judge what is read or heard.

So, what I mean when I say that parents need this book is not that they need this particular book, but that they need the information it offers.

If you read a lot, you will read a lot of facts; you will also read a lot of personal opinion.

There are the Coverdell ESA facts; and there are the personal opinions of those who write about Coverdell accounts.

There are stock-market facts; and there are the personal opinions of those who write about stocks.

In other words, even though a lot of what you might read or hear is accurate, some is not; and even if something is "true," it might not apply to your unique situation.

One of the best examples is the advice offered in financial periodicals. The advice in any week's or month's issue may be great—meaning that it is both accurate and useful. The problem is that periodicals publish new issues every week or month, and there is little reason for customers to buy new issues if the advice doesn't change. The same is true for newspaper columns. As a result, because periodicals do their best to offer new ideas and advice in every issue, last week's "10 Best Investments of All Time" is replaced by this week's "10 Best Investments of All Time."

The problem is, if you followed last week's advice, what do you do this week? Or next month? Or next year? That is why it is important to have an understanding of the fundamentals that do not change week to week.

That is why one of the major purposes of this book is to help you judge what you read.

The Big-Time Plan

IF YOU READ EVERYTHING up to this point, you may be getting a headache.

Which is why this is a good time to review it all, before going on.

1. Your Big-Time Plan

Step 1
Decide to save money for your child.

Step 2
Find an easy place to save "loose" money—a shoebox, paper bag, or whatever. Put the gift-money your child receives in the box and add your loose change whenever you can.

Step 3
Open a Coverdell ESA so that you can up to $2,000 a year in specific investments. If you do not want to make specific investments on your own, you do not need a Coverdell account.

Step 4
Open a 529 (EdVest) savings plan and make periodic contributions to the account. This account could be the main savings and investment account for your child. And there may be a time when you want to transfer the funds in a Coverdell ESA into your 529 plan.

Step 5

Set up automatic or periodic contributions to your account.

Step 6

If it makes sense for you and your family, open a Roth IRA. Check with an expert before you do this, and certainly before you count on using it as your child's main education fund.

Step 7

If you want to save and invest money for your children for something other than college expenses, you should not use your 529 savings plan. You do not want more money in this account than you plan on spending for college.

Step 8

If you want to invest for your children outside a college account, do not set up a custodial account or trust fund without talking with an expert about your personal situation. Neither offers any benefits for most families. And each will cost you money while taking away your control of the funds.

2. Managing a 529 savings plan

After you open a 529 savings plan, you can make contributions to the account, but you cannot make individual investment decisions with the money in the account. Instead, you have to choose from the "portfolio options" offered by the fund's manager in your state, normally a large bank.

Even though you cannot make individual investment decisions, you should have a basic understanding of how investments work; either to help decide how you want the funds in your 529 account managed or to understand what you can do with a Coverdell ESA or with money invested outside a college savings plan.

What You Should Know About Investing

ANYONE WHO HAS a Coverdell ESA and/or a 529 savings plan and/or a Roth IRA, should know a little about the investment markets, because there are decisions you have to make, even if it is simply to choose which of the many 529 investment bundles is best for your family. If you are investing on your own, you should probably know even more.

The problem is: investment markets can be confusing or boring, or both. But, boring or not, everyone should understand the basics of investing.

So, here they are.

1. Own versus loan

Investment writers like to separate investments into either "own" or "loan" categories.[11]

The idea is that when you make an investment, you are either buying ownership of an asset (which may give you a share of future profits) or making a loan to someone.

If you buy gold or common stocks or part of an oil well, you are hoping that the value of what you "own" will increase over time. If it is gold, you hope that the price of gold will rise. If it is a share of XYZ stock, you hope that the price of that particular stock will increase. If it is a share in an oil well, you hope that your cut of future profits will be greater than your investment.[12]

When you buy "debt instruments," such as bonds or CDs, you are actually making a loan. When you buy a bond or CD, it means that someone is borrowing money. In return, they promise to pay back the loan plus interest. In some cases, the interest you receive is fixed. In others, it varies over time.

Sometimes you receive interest payments on an annual or semi-annual basis (e.g. regular bonds and notes).

Sometimes all the interest accumulates and is paid when the asset reaches maturity (e.g. zero coupon bonds, CDs, Series EE savings bonds).

And sometimes the life of the asset is so short that even though all the interest is due at maturity, it seems as though you are constantly being paid (e.g. three-month Treasury bills).

---

[11] This is investment-industry jargon.

[12] I am not going to discuss the old idea of "tax-advantaged" investments in oil wells, or any other schemes designed to beat the IRS. Existing tax laws virtually eliminated those tax breaks. Today, you have to make investments that return real profits—not tax write-offs.

2. Risk

Any saving-and-investment plan must take account of the tax laws that can affect which plans are "best," as well as which investments we might choose.

But—and this is truly important—focusing on tax laws and potential investment returns can lead to taking risks you may not be able to afford.

I believe that your child's financial plan is so important that it should minimize risk, meaning that it should contain the smallest possible chance of loss.

The purpose of your child's account is so crucial that the potential rewards from winning on a risky investment are not likely to outweigh the consequences of losing.

Of course, you can choose to ignore my minimizing-risk rule if:

You are wealthy enough so that your future plans would not be affected by significant losses.

The total portfolio value exceeds the projected future needs of your children; and the risky investments (with potentially high return) are made with "extra" funds.

But before I give you a misleading impression of "no risk," let me explain what I mean.

First, risk is a relative, not an absolute, concept. There are no absolutely risk-free investments.

An investment with a guaranteed return of principal and interest means you will not lose your money. But it does not mean you are guaranteed to beat inflation.

So the idea of risk must be handled carefully.

Some people are more afraid of inflation than of the possibility of losing their funds in an investment that turns sour. Many of these people believe that the most risk free investments are precious metals or other "tangible" assets whose prices tend to rise with the rate of inflation.

My belief is that the possibility of being hurt by an unexpected runaway inflation is much smaller than the possibility of losing money on gold, silver, or even a major "blue chip" stock. At the same time, it is unlikely that inflation will be completely eliminated in the foreseeable future. Therefore, your plans should account for an almost certain two to three percent rate of inflation.

Second, being "risk free" does not mean earning a poor return. In fact, the future value of your total portfolio can be greater if you make only investments that "can't lose" rather than hitting some winners and discarding some losers.

Third, once you have built your child's portfolio to a level that is expected to meet your (his or her) future needs, you may decide to add some riskier investments that offer potentially higher returns.

That is fine. My only reservation is that when you invest in assets that can lose as well as gain value, it is not always easy to be successful.

It is one thing to say, "OK, now it's time to make some real money." It is another to actually do it.

Obviously, the decision is up to you.

But I want to make two strong recommendations:

1) Keep your child's account as risk free as possible, at least until it reaches a relatively high total value.

2) Even after building a successful portfolio for your child, think carefully before jumping into a "great deal" with "unlimited potential."

But a child's account is not the place to try to "hit it big." It should be a place to do the best you can for your children, within your abilities and within the risk limits that you can afford.

Investment Du Jour

GARRISON KEILLOR'S "mythical little town that time forgot"—Lake Wobegon—has a café. The cafe's menu features "hot dish du jour."

If you grew up in the Midwest (as I did), surrounded by hot dishes at every gathering, the idea of a menu with "hot dish du jour" is pretty funny. But when it comes to investing, especially for our children, it is not funny to see people getting caught up in fads, or ordering the "investment of the day." One of the main purposes of this book is to help you establish a simple, workable, profitable saving and investment plan for your children. I cannot say that sensible new ideas will not come along. I can say that if you have a solid plan in place, and a good understanding of a few basic investments, there is not much chance you will be taken in by the hype that surrounds each new pie-in-the-sky idea.

That is because you will have a benchmark. You will be able to compare whatever new idea is being pushed to something real. And if you can do that, you can decide for yourself what is and is not sensible for you.

Those who are most likely to fall for a "too good to be true" scheme are those who are doing nothing. They are the ones who are looking for the one big score to bail them out.

But if you have a plan in place, the only ideas that will make sense are those that can do better than what you are already doing.

Of course, few "new ideas" are really new. Sometimes, truly new opportunities do occur, opportunities that did not exist in the past. But, most of the time, what you will see is someone "rediscovering" the "incredible benefits" of an investment idea that has been around for many years.

Therefore, I want to give you a little information on the most common investments. I will try to be as straightforward as I can. But there is no way to hide my opinion of risk in a child's portfolio. At the same time, I do not want to give you a negative impression of any legitimate investment.

My major concern with many "great-idea" investments is that they require a lot of knowledge and a large time commitment if you are going to be successful.

Almost any legitimate investment can make sense for an adult portfolio, if you are willing and able to put in the time to learn about it and to follow it on a daily basis.

But few of us have the time to become "experts" on investments just so we can include them in a child's portfolio.

1. Investments that are loans.

Money market mutual funds, Certificates of Deposit, zero-coupon Treasury bonds, Series EE savings bonds, and regular Treasury bonds, notes, and bills are investments that offer guaranteed returns.[13] You know exactly how much each will be worth at a given future date, and the dollar returns are guaranteed.

Each is either issued by the United States government or insured by a trustworthy source. Therefore, you know you will get your money back—with interest.

But, as I already explained, whenever you put money into a long-term, interest-bearing asset, you may have to worry about inflation. Buying a long-term bond that pays five percent interest may sound good when the inflation rate is one or two percent. But, if the inflation rate jumps to eight or nine percent, your investment will be losing real value each year, meaning that the purchasing power of your investment will decline day by day. If that happens and you try to sell your bonds before maturity, you will also have to take a loss.[14]

The truth, however, is that there is virtually no possibility that the real inflation rate in the United States will remain above three or four percent for a number of years.

---

[13] I am ignoring corporate bonds, because they are too risky for a child's account. Unlike the federal government, a private company may default on its bonds. If you remember, one of the "financial instruments" in the middle of the 2008 financial meltdown were "credit default swaps," which, in simple terms, were bets on whether or not companies would default on their bonds.

[14] When the inflation rate increases, so do market interest rates; and if you want to (or have to) sell bonds before maturity, you will receive less than the maturity value.

2. A few questions and answers

Q: Who issues bonds, notes, and bills?

A: Institutions (not individuals) that want to borrow money. Corporations, government municipalities, public utilities, school districts, counties, states, the federal government, and federal agencies.

Q: Why do they borrow money?

A: To meet current expenses, or to expand.

Corporations can raise money in three ways: take it from retained earnings (if they have any), sell stock (which gives up some ownership of the company), or borrow (sell bonds). Part of an owner's or manager's job is to decide which method is best. Sometimes, the best choice is to borrow.

State and local governments have two ways to raise money: tax or borrow (sell bonds).

The federal government can also raise money with taxes or by selling bonds. But there is a third choice on the federal level. If the federal government sells bonds to raise money, the Federal Reserve Bank (the central bank of the United States) can buy some or all of those bonds with new money it creates by writing Federal Reserve checks.

And that is where the possibility of inflation comes in. If the federal government finances its deficit spending by selling a lot of bonds, and the Federal Reserve buys a lot of bonds by creating new money, the rate of inflation may increase.

Q: What is the difference between bonds, notes, and bills?

A: The time to maturity when they are originally issued. Treasury bills are issued to come due in three, six, or twelve months. Treasury notes are issued to mature in one to ten years.

Q: Do you have to hold a bond or note until maturity?

A: No. Bills, notes, and bonds are marketable, which means they can be sold to someone else after their initial purchase. You can buy a 30-year bond and sell it whenever you want. You cannot sell it back to the issuer until maturity. But you can sell it to another investor.

You can also purchase a 20-year bond that was originally issued 15-years ago, which means it will mature in five years even though it is technically called a 20-year bond. If you hold it until maturity, it will be redeemed at face value (normally $1,000 or $5,000) by the issuing agency or corporation. If you want to sell it before it reaches maturity, you can do that as well. You can buy and sell bonds, notes, and bills whenever you want.

As a result, you can purchase 30-year bonds that will mature at any times you choose—in 18-years, 19-years, or whenever.

Q: Is there any advantage to purchasing original issues?

A: Not unless you want to lock in current interest rates for as long as possible. Then you would buy bonds with the longest possible time to maturity, which would be original issues.

Q: Can I always buy and sell bonds at the same price?

A: No. The face value of a bond is what you will receive when the bond is redeemed at maturity. A $1,000 30-year Treasury bond or a $1,000 zero-coupon bond will be worth $1,000 at maturity.

But if you buy or sell such bonds after they are originally issued, the price you pay or receive depends on current market interest rates. For example, if you buy a new 30-year Treasury bond paying five percent interest, you will pay $1,000 for the bond. And in 30-years, you will get your $1,000 back.

In the meantime, you will receive $50 each year, which is five percent interest, until the bond matures or until you sell it.

What happens if market interest rates rise so that new bonds are issued to pay eight percent interest, or $80 a year? Your bond will still pay only $50 a year, because when bonds are issued, the dollar value of the annual dividend is fixed to match the original interest rate. Therefore, if you want to sell your bond, no one will give you $1,000 for it because for $1,000 they can buy a bond that pays $80 a year instead of $50.

If you want to sell your bond, you will have to settle for less than $1,000.

Of course, if you hold it until maturity, you will always receive $1,000—no matter what happens to market interest rates.

Q: What is the best way to avoid getting stuck with a loss due to rising interest rates?

A: Buy bonds that you expect to hold until maturity. If you want a bond that you can sell in 19-years (for example, when your one year old will be twenty), buy one that will mature in 19-years, which is when you will need the money. That way you know exactly what interest you will earn and exactly what the bond will be worth when you sell it, because you will sell it at maturity.

Do not buy a new 30-year bond and plan on selling it in the open market in 19-years. If you do, you might have to sell it at a loss, which could negate a large part of the interest you earned over the years.

Of course, if interest rates fall after you buy your bond, you can sell for a profit!

Q: How do I get the highest interest?

A: Interest, or yield, is a function of two factors: risk and (sometimes) time to maturity. The greater the risk of possible default, the higher the yield will be (which is why government bonds pay a lower rate of interest than corporate bonds). And the longer the time to maturity, the higher the yield will normally be.

Sometimes, because of economic circumstances, short-term yields can be greater than long-term yields.

Q: When is the interest paid?

A: Treasury bills, Series EE savings bonds, and zero-coupon bonds pay all their interest at maturity. Standard notes and bonds pay interest twice a year

Q: Which are the "best" bonds and notes to buy?

A: That depends on a number of factors: yield, risk, expectations of future inflation and future interest rates, the size of the investment you want to make, and what makes sense to you. I like zero-coupon Treasury bonds. Some people will not buy them because they refuse to pay yearly taxes on accumulating interest that they will not receive until the bonds mature. This is not an issue if zero-coupon bonds are held in Coverdell or 529 accounts, because the interest is tax-free.

In any case, the choices can be overwhelming. Corporate versus government issues. Taxable government bonds versus tax-free municipal bonds. Short-term versus long-term issues. Interest-bearing bonds versus zero-coupon bonds. Treasury bonds versus government agency bonds. Treasury bills versus money market funds. New issues versus secondary purchases.

Whatever you pick, you can find someone who will argue that it is the best choice, which should not be surprising; because each offers something the others do not. Therefore, each might be "best" for someone. If that were not true, all the choices would not exist. Those that serve no special purpose would disappear from the market, because no one would buy them. So, if someone tries to tell you that one choice is best for everyone, he or she is wrong. And if someone tries to tell you that one choice is absolutely worthless, he is wrong too.

As I already said, if something exists, there is a reason for it to do so. The question is: What is best for a given purpose?

Zero-Coupon Treasury bonds

Zero-Coupon Treasury bonds are U.S. government bonds that do not pay yearly dividends. Instead, they are sold at a "discount"—meaning that the price you pay to buy them is less than the price you receive when they mature. The difference between what you pay and what you receive is the total compounded interest on your investment.

The typical zero-coupon Treasury bond has a maturity value of $1,000. That means you receive $1,000 for each bond when it "matures" or comes due.

How much does each bond cost? That depends on two factors: how long it will be held before it matures and current interest rates. Zero-coupon bonds that pay a five percent yield will double in value every twelve years. That means you can buy a bond for a new baby for $250 and cash it in for $1,000 when he or she is 24 years old. The $750 gain is the accumulated interest on your $250 investment.

You can purchase zero-coupon Treasury bonds that will mature whenever you want, from next year to 30-years in the future.[15]

So you can select bonds that will come due as your child reaches certain ages. Some can mature at age 18, others at ages 19, 20, 21, and so on. The longer you plan on waiting before collecting the $1,000, the less you pay for each bond.[16]

---

[15] Of course, this is true for all bonds.

[16] Why would you want a bond that matures when your child is 24? There are at least two reasons. One is that some children will still be in school when they are 24. The other is that the money can be used to pay off student loans after your child graduates.

And the higher interest rates are, the lower the price of each bond will be when you buy it.[17]

There are two positive things about Zero-coupon Treasury bonds and one negative.

The positives are:

Because they are sold at a discount, zero-coupon bonds can be purchased for a few hundred dollars, rather than $1,000 for a bond that pays dividends.

More important is that zero-coupon bonds pay compound interest, which means interest is earned on interest already paid, which is not the case for bonds that pay annual dividends (or coupons).

The negative is:

You have to pay taxes on the accumulating interest, even though no interest is actually received.

In terms of a portfolio for your children, you can take advantage of the positives and avoid the negative if you purchase zero-coupon bonds through a tax-advantaged account, because if the bonds are held in a tax-free account, the interest accumulates tax free at a compound rate.

---

[17] The price you pay to purchase a zero-coupon bond is the dollar value that, at current interest rates, will grow to be worth $1,000 at maturity.

If, for some reason, you do not have a Coverdell ESA or a 529 (EdVest) plan, or if you want to purchase zero-coupon bonds outside a tax-advantaged savings plan, it is possible to have your shoebox money purchase one or more zero-coupon Treasury bonds each year—at least until your child is nine or ten years old. After that, there will be fewer years between his or her age and the time you will most likely want to cash-in his or her bonds. And the shorter the time such bonds are held, the less they can appreciate.

As long as you purchase only U.S. Treasury Bonds, there is no risk of default. You do, or course, face a risk if you have to sell your bonds before maturity. If interest rates rise sharply after you buy, and you have to sell before maturity, you will not be able to sell your bonds for what you paid for them.

But if you know you are going to hold each bond until maturity, there is no reason to worry about its fluctuating market value. No matter what happens to interest rates after you buy, you will receive $1,000 for each bond held until maturity.

Tax-free zero-coupon bonds also exist; they are issued by municipalities. But they are not risk free.

In summary, zero-coupon Treasury bonds can be a good choice for a child's portfolio. They let you lock in compound interest for many years. There is no risk of default. You know exactly how much each bond will be worth at maturity ($1,000). You can choose bonds with maturity dates that correspond to when you expect to spend the money. You can purchase zero-coupon bonds for relatively low prices. And you earn compound interest at a locked-in rate—a true advantage if you buy zero-coupon Treasury bonds when interest rates are relatively high.

But remember:

* You do not want to buy zero-coupon bonds or any other long-term, interest-bearing investment if you expect interest rates to rise. It is better to keep your funds invested in short-term, interest-bearing accounts until rates increase. Then lock in the higher rates for the long run.

* If interest rates rise unexpectedly after you buy zero-coupon bonds, it is not the end of the world. It means that you missed a chance to do better. But that is not the worst thing that can happen.

* The one true problem with rising interest rates is that they lower the market value of your bond. Therefore, you want to buy zero-coupon bonds with maturity dates that correspond to the times you want to cash them in. That way, you can avoid the problem of having to sell at a loss if interest rates increase after you buy.

Series EE Savings Bonds

Series EE bonds are a type of zero-coupon bond, which means they are purchased at a discount. A $50 bond is purchased for $25. A $100 bond for $50, and so on.

At one time, Series EE savings bonds were one of the worst investments you could make. Then they were one of the best—if used for education expenses. Now, because of Coverdell and 529 savings plans, as well as Roth IRAs, they have limited value.

As with most investments offered by the federal government, the rules can change.

The current (meaning while I am writing this) rules are:

Series EE bonds pay a fixed rate of interest, equal to 90 percent of the average return on ten year Treasury Bonds. (A few years ago, they paid a variable rate of interest tied to five-year bonds.)

The interest is compounded (added to the value of the bond) semi-annually.

Series EE bonds have to be held at least one year before they earn any interest.

If you hold a Series EE bond for 20 years, the government guarantees that it will double in value. That means there is a minimum rate of return of about 3.6 percent, which is not bad. The reason the guaranteed rate of return is not bad is because all the earnings are tax-free if used for education expenses.

Unfortunately, to receive the guaranteed minimum return, you have to hold a Series EE bond for 20 years. If you sell before that, you receive only the return that was offered when the bond was purchased, which was 3.5 percent a while ago but is now only about one percent. And the rate does not change, no matter how high market rates go after you buy a bond.

The only advantage of Series EE savings bonds, other than that they can be purchased for as little as $25 (with no fee), is that they offer one of the few remaining education tax breaks outside Coverdell ESAs, 529 plans, and Roth IRAs. If you buy Series EE Treasury bonds and use the proceeds for higher education expenses (tuition and books), the interest might be tax-free. You can use the money for your education, your spouse's education, or your child's education.

The reason the earnings "might" be tax-free is that there is a "catch" to the tax-free offer. The tax-free status is a function of your income. Currently, the entire interest is tax-free if your adjusted gross income is less than $67,100 ($100,650 for a joint return) in the year the bonds are cashed (not when they are purchased). There is a sliding scale that applies taxes to taxes on the interest if your adjusted gross income exceeds $67,000 ($130,650 for a joint return). And, if your income is more than $82,100 for a single return or $130,650 for a joint return, you pay taxes on all the interest.

You also have to remember that if the money is to be used for your child's education, the bonds cannot be in your child's name to qualify for tax-free status. They must be in the name of either one or both parents.

Series EE bonds used to be called "education" bonds, because they offered one of the few tax-breaks available to parents saving for future education expenses.

You can buy Series EE bonds at commercial banks, savings institutions, or through many Payroll Savings Plans for as little as $25. And there are no fees or commissions.

But you should be careful to keep records of all such bonds. Otherwise, you may run into a lot of red tape when you want to claim the tax exclusion.

Your local IRS office will tell you what records to keep. (Essentially, you use IRS form 8818 to record each bond's serial number, issue date, and face value when cashed. Later you will need receipts from an educational institution.)

And interest earned on Series EE savings bonds is always exempt from state and local income taxes.

Although Series EE bonds offer some benefits, most parents will be better off concentrating on investments made in Coverdell ESAs, 529 plans, and/or Roth IRAs.

Regular government bonds

The standard government bond pays semi-annual dividends. Instead of automatically reinvesting the interest on you initial investment, the interest is given to you twice a year. Then you have to figure out what to do with it.

As a rule, the time to buy bonds of any kind is when interest rates are relatively high. If rates are expected to rise in the future, you should wait before making a long-term, commitment. Keep your money earning short-term interest until long-term rates are high enough to justify locking up your money. And remember—it is locking up your money, because if interest rates increase after you buy a bond, you are stuck with it, unless you are willing to sell at a loss. But, no matter how high long-term interest rates go, your return on normal bonds is not compounded. How much difference does compound interest make? A lot, here is an example that does not really apply to a child's account. But it is interesting anyway.

When George Washington and his troops were huddled at Valley Forge, they had run out of supplies and money.

Washington wrote to a wealthy citizen, who lived nearby, and explained that unless funds could be raised, the army would have to be disbanded. This citizen apparently gave Washington $450,000 in cash and supplies. It was all he had. But it was enough to keep the army together; and to give Washington's army the chance to win our independence. But the loan was never repaid. And the descendants of the lender, who died penniless, tried to sue the government for the money it owed them.

Using a six percent rate of interest, which was the rate at the time of the Revolutionary War, by 1990 the value of the loan was more than $140 billion—if it were compounded daily. If it were compounded annually, it was worth $90 billion.

That is a lot of money. And a big difference.

So if you choose to invest in bonds that pay semi-annual dividends, which means the interest is not compounded at all, you should have a good idea of what you will do with the interest you receive.

Why worry about what to do with the interest on regular notes and bonds?

Because that is the return on your investment. If you buy a bond for $1,000, you get your $1,000 back at maturity. The only gains are the yearly interest payments. So, what you do with the dividends is crucial to making regular bonds a good investment.

2. A few more questions and answers

Q: Should I buy short-term or long-term interest-bearing investments?

A: I can explain this one to you, but I cannot give you a simple recommendation. That is because the question of short-term versus long-term depends on expectations of future interest rates.

If you think interest rates are relatively low (and will be increasing), you do not want to make an investment that locks in the current rate. You do not want to buy zero-coupon bonds or regular long-term bonds. You want to leave your funds in an account that earns short-term rates and let the money be continually reinvested at higher and higher rates. Then, when you think rates are high enough, switch your funds to a long-term investment that will lock-in those yields.

If you think interest rates are relatively high (and will be falling), you want to lock-in the current rate while you can. You want to buy long-term zero-coupon bonds instead of leaving your funds in short-term assets.

Very simply, if you expect interest rates to fall, buy long-term bonds. If you expect interest rates to rise, keep you funds in a money-market account. (That does not mean selling long-term bonds you already own. What we are talking about here is what to do with new money added to an account.)

It sounds simple. But even the top experts have trouble forecasting future interest rates. So never hesitate to talk to your broker and to others to see what they think—and why.

Whenever someone gives you financial advice and/or predictions, always ask: Why?

Q: What about inflation?

A: Inflation is a tricky issue. During periods of rising inflation, interest rates have to increase as well, because it makes no sense to let someone use your money if what you eventually get back will not buy as much as it could have bought when you made the loan.

Therefore, if you buy a long-term bond at a non-inflationary interest rate and then inflation picks up, your bond will be a "bad" investment during the period of inflation. But as inflation cools off, your bond becomes a good investment again.

Therefore, if you buy a 30-year bond and hold it for 30-years, there will be times when you will be disappointed—because you could have done better if you had waited. And there will be times when you will be glad that you bought when you did.

On the other hand, short-term interest rates—the rates you earn on 3-month Treasury bills, CDs, or money-market funds will normally be above the inflation rate. These short-term rates have to make sense when the investment is made. Otherwise, no one will buy them.

There are times, however, when a bad economy creates so much fear of loss that investors are willing to accept short-term interest rates that are below the rate of inflation in return for safety—the guaranteed safe-keeping of their money by the federal government.

So, if you are truly afraid of inflation, here is a three-step plan.

1) Leave your money in money-market funds or CDs.

2) Do not make substantial long-term, interest-bearing investments until interest rates rise to what you believe are adequately high levels. (Which would be when you expect the inflation rate to decrease.)

Normally, the highest interest rates occur while the money supply is being contracted to reduce an unacceptable rate of inflation. So if inflation does become a serious issue, wait until it is clear that the money supply is being restricted. The lower the quantity of money available for loans, the higher interest rates will be. That is the time to switch from short-term interest-bearing assets to long-term bonds.

3) Consider buying tangible assets, such as gold, silver, and collectibles. Some people believe that our persistent inflation rate (even if it is relatively low) makes such investments the best choices of all. But that is a tough claim to back up. It is easy to find periods of time when gold or silver or certain collectibles outperformed all other investments. The problem is that tangible assets, as well as stocks, can lose as well as gain value.

Q: How can I calculate the return on investments that yield compound interest—such as zero-coupon and Series EE bonds?

A: You can use the "rule of 72" to get a quick answer.

If you divide the number 72 by any interest rate, the answer is the number of years it will take for an investment to double in value. If you divide the number 72 by any number of years, the answer is the compound interest rate you would have to receive in order for an investment to double in value in that many years.

For example, if the current interest rate on CDs, money-market funds or zero-coupon bonds is six percent, dividing six into 72 gives you 12. That means the investment will double in value every twelve years.

If you invest $250 at a six percent compounded annual rate of return, the $250 will be worth $500 in twelve years. And in twelve more years, it will double again—to $1,000.

That is how zero-coupon bonds appreciate.

Money-market rates work the same—except for the fact that money-market rates change over time while zero-coupon bond rates are locked-in for the life of the bond.

The point is: You can buy a zero-coupon Treasury bond for $500 at five percent interest and know it will be worth $1,000 in twelve years.

Or you can let the money accumulate in a money-market fund. If rates stay at five percent, it too will be worth $1,000 in 12 years. If rates rise, it will be worth more. If rates fall, it will be worth less than $1,000.

In either case, however, the annual appreciation or interest must be reported as income—either in your child's name or yours (unless the bonds are being held in a Coverdell ESA or 529 plan or a Roth IRA).

Series EE savings bonds are different.

With Series EE bond, the annual appreciation does not have to be reported as income.

And if, when the bonds are cashed, the money is used for education, the interest will be totally tax-free. (If you meet the income limitations.)

3. Investments you own

Common stocks

Many advisors recommend common stocks for a child's portfolio. The reasons are clear:

1) Unlike interest-bearing securities, common stocks have unlimited potential; with stocks, the sky is the limit.

2) Taxes on appreciation are not due until the stock is sold. Therefore, stocks can be transferred to a child before they are sold, which means the capital gains would be taxed at the child's rate.

Those are good arguments for anyone who invests outside a Coverdell ESA, 529 plan, or Roth IRA.

But because taxes on appreciation are not an issue with Coverdell or 529 accounts or Roth IRAs, the real issue is profits—meaning, how good are you at picking stocks?

If a stock analyst could unfailingly pick stocks that only appreciate, he or she would be the most famous stock-picker of all time. But that is exactly what you can do with government bonds. With government bonds, there is absolutely no chance you will pick a loser. (Except, as I said, if we are overrun with a high rate of inflation.)

Meanwhile, no one has ever been able to select only winning stocks. No one ever will. And the common error many people make when considering stocks as the primary investment for a child's portfolio is to get caught up in greed, which happens when we look at the big winners and ignore the big losers.

But I do not want to tell anyone to avoid stocks.

If you are a successful stock-market investor, or have expert advice, you will not want to pass up the chance to do the best you can for your children. But if you are not an experienced and successful stock-market investor, the fact that you are investing for your children will not guarantee success. It is possible to prepare a scenario that makes any investment market look like a fantastic opportunity. All you have to do is round up a bunch of historical numbers, pick the right time period to cover, and concentrate on the winners while ignoring the losers.

Picking a "winning" stock is a great experience. Not only can you make a bundle of money. You also get a big boost to your ego. I am sure that anyone who has ever looked at the stock market remembers a stock they should have bought—a stock that went through the roof. But most of us forget about all the stocks we thought about buying that went nowhere but down.

The one rule of thumb for investing in stocks—and every broker will (or should) tell it to you is: "Only invest money you can afford to lose." For most of us, the money in our children's portfolios is not money we can afford to lose.

Mutual funds

Mutual funds collect money from a large number of individual investors and use that money to buy a large number of different securities. The idea behind a mutual fund is that by purchasing a wide variety of securities, the risk of loss is reduced. That is normally true.

The main idea behind mutual funds, however, is that because the stock market tends to increase over time, a broad selection of individual stocks will do at least as well as the overall market. It won't do as well as the biggest winners, but it won't do a poorly as the biggest losers either. Therefore, even though there will always be periods of declining prices, good mutual funds tend to appreciate over time, and the better ones appreciate more than the market.

That is why mutual funds advertise their past achievements in one of two ways: How well they did compared to the market, or how well they did compared to other mutual funds.

Of course, neither measurement is a guarantee for the future. A mutual fund that returned a good profit last year may have done so my choosing stocks that others passed up. But in a cyclical world, the stocks that were last year's big winners could be this year's or next year's big losers. Even so, for most families, mutual funds are a better choice than individual stocks.

The typical mutual fund tends to do a little better than the stock market (as measured by an index such at the Dow Jones Industrial Average) when the market is rising. But mutual funds can do worse than the market when the market is falling. Therefore, if stock prices were some sort of "perfect" cycle, the gains would be washed out by the losses. But over time the stock market tends to cycle higher. As a result, mutual funds tend to gain value over time, as well.

If you invest in mutual funds for your children, chances are the investment will be held long enough to gain from the upward trend of the stock market. But if you were someone who had planned on using you mutual fund investments in 1988 or 1989, or 2008, 2009, or 2010, you would have been in for an unpleasant surprise.

Therefore, I caution you to put the "track records" that indicate past performance in perspective before deciding that mutual funds are your best choice.

You should also be aware of the fact that there are many different kinds of mutual funds. So far, I have been referring to mutual funds that invest in a broad range of stocks. But many funds invest in specialized stocks. Some invest primarily in "growth" stocks—stocks that are expected to gain in value rather than yield high dividends. Others select only foreign stocks, precious metals stocks, income stocks (dividends instead of growth), and so on. Some invest in bonds or short-term securities. Some choose combinations.

There are so many mutual funds that no matter which market category you pick, you can find a mutual fund that specializes in that area. Some funds charge relatively high fees—both to buy and sell, as well as to cover annual management costs. Others have no fees for buying and selling. But almost all have a built-in annual charge. And the charges can be high enough to wipe out a considerable part of your gains. So check carefully before you act. If you are on any investment mailing lists, you have probably received advertisements from "experts" who claim they can (for a fee) help you earn a good return by telling you when to switch from one type of mutual fund to another. That is not a totally false claim. As economic conditions change, some economic sectors will do better than others. But trying to beat the market by switching back and forth is a tough path to follow over the years.

If you believe that the stock market offers potential returns that outweigh the returns on interest-bearing securities, then I suggest you follow the old standby investment plan. Invest a given amount of money each month or every two or three months (but stick to your schedule) in a mutual fund that matches the market.

Instead of trying to beat the market, just go along with it. And do not plan on selling until some time in the future.

If you follow such a plan, you will buy more stocks when stock prices are low and less when stock prices are high. You will not lose by trying to guess the tops and bottoms of cycles. And you will accumulate value that matches the market itself.

Over time, your investment should return a good profit.

But it will not be a lot higher than what you could earn if you invest in government securities—especially if you buy zero-coupon bonds when interest rates are high.

And it could be lower, because there is no guarantee in the stock market.

Is it "fair" to keep saying there are no guarantees in stocks? I think it is. In the first place, there are some guarantees when you invest in government securities. In the second place, when you are investing for your child's future, you should look for all the guarantees you can get.

Precious metals

If you are scared to death of inflation, you will probably end up buying some tangible assets. Precious metals and gold and silver coins, are marketed heavily in this country. And anyone who is afraid of inflation is going to listen to the sales pitch:

* People from around the world have chosen to put funds into precious metals for many years.

* Gold and silver have helped many people through times of economic disaster and political upheaval.

* And precious metals have appreciated faster than the rate of inflation.

It is a pretty good sales pitch. But the argument is not really applicable to America.

America is not in danger of either political or economic collapse. Nor is America in danger of falling victim to a hyperinflation.

On the other hand, it looks as though we may be stuck with a one to three percent average rate of inflation for years to come. And a one to three percent rate of inflation is enough to distort markets and affect the returns on every investment.

Therefore, I understand the appeal of tangible assets.

But it is important to understand the complexities in the tangible assets markets before investing any money.

There are two broad categories of tangible assets: Those bought as collectibles (hopefully by people who appreciate them for what they are, rather than by someone who hopes to make a quick buck) and those bought as strict investments.

Truly rare coins fit into the first category.

Gold and silver bullion belong in the second.

Then there are the overlaps—gold and silver coins, for example, that are not truly "rare," but are scarce enough to command prices above their bullion content.

Although the highest prices obviously go to the true collectibles, the average investor has no business buying collectibles as an investment. The true collector may make a large profit on his or her collection. But it was a collection bought with knowledge and interest. The profit, if any, is an extra.

Unfortunately, there are many national telemarketers selling "collectibles" as investments. And it is difficult to dismiss the appeal of million-dollar coins. Even so, I recommend that you keep your greed in check and stay away from such sales pitches.

If you do not have the required knowledge, you will not know what you are buying. And all collectibles are not equal when it comes to future potential. Also, there are large markups on many collectibles, both when you buy and when you sell. It is not uncommon to pay a 20 percent markdown from retail when you sell.

Viewed as a retail business, such profit margins may not seem out of line. But as investments, such collectibles are questionable. As a rule of thumb, the retail prices of such collectibles have to double for you to break even after paying your buy and sell "commissions."

An equally significant problem is that few of us can judge the quality of high-priced collectibles. With rare coins, for example, a slightly higher quality can cause the price to double or triple. That is not a problem for an expert who can tell the difference. But if you are not an expert, you may overpay. And if you do, you may never get your original investment back.

So, if you want to add some tangible assets to your child's portfolio, I recommend you stay with bullion, or with gold and silver coins that are priced according to their bullion content.

I prefer gold to either silver or platinum, because gold is mainly an investment metal. Silver and platinum are used as industrial metals and their prices can be affected by many unforeseen economic circumstances.

Gold is also the most international precious metal. And it can be purchased in small bars or in newly minted coins that are not intended for circulation (not "real" money).

The larger the size of the bar or coin, the lower the premium. But all gold investments carry some premium over the "spot price" that is reported in the daily paper. The spot price is really a wholesale price.

Although you can calculate the markup over the spot price on a one-ounce bar and a ten-ounce bar, the difference is not of much significance. It stays the same when you buy and sell. What matters more is the price difference between dealers. And that can vary by a wide margin. So if you want to buy gold, get prices from a number of reputable dealers before you buy.

But remember, as the "premium" increases—meaning that the markup over the spot price of gold gets larger—you are either getting into collectibles, which you want to avoid unless you have help form an expert you can trust, or you may be getting a bad deal.

I have to tell you that it makes me nervous to discuss precious metals at all. Not because they are a terrible idea. But because I do not believe the average person should put a large percentage of a child's portfolio into precious metals. And because I know that if you buy any precious metals or coins at all, you are likely to run into a high-pressure sales pitch to buy more. These salesmen can be convincing, especially if you are legitimately worried about the consequences of inflation.

On the other hand, if you want to become an expert on precious metals or collectibles, such as rare coins, read more than one book before making major decisions. Many books are written by dealers and do not give you an unbiased view of the subject.

These are interesting markets. But they take time to learn. And unless you are already an expert, you should put only a small percentage of your child's money into such investments.

Annuities

Annuities are normally sold as a retirement investment—as a vehicle that earns interest while deferring taxes. But with so many older parents with young children, annuities are also being marketed as an investment possibility for children.

Essentially, annuities are simple.

You buy one, normally for $1,000 to $10,000, and earn interest that is not paid and not taxed until sometime in the future.

Because taxes are deferred, annuities are often called "tax shelters." But I think that is being a little hopeful. It is one thing to discuss the possibility of deferring taxes. It is another to claim that doing so will result in lower taxes.

For some reason, it is commonly assumed that if you put off taxes on some income until you are retired, you will definitely pay a lower tax rate on that income

Sometimes that is true. Sometimes it is not. Many retired people have incomes that are higher than they had while they were working, because of pensions and investments. They can, therefore, end up paying a higher, not a lower, tax rate. Also, no one knows what the tax rates will be in 15 or 20 years. So how can anyone be certain that it is a good idea to pay taxes later, rather than now?

There are other, more serious, problems with annuities.

1) Annuities are not risk free. They are issued by private corporations—insurance companies. Therefore, there is a risk of default. To remove that risk, many annuities are now insured. But, as in any market, less risk means a lower return.

2) If you withdraw any money from an annuity before age 59 1/2, it is taxed fully. Plus, you have to pay a ten percent penalty tax on the earnings withdrawn. Therefore, if you are planning on using the earnings from an annuity for your child, be sure you will be 59 ½ when you want to spend the money

3) Annuities pay a return set by the insurance company. The first year's yield is always fairly high. After that, you have no idea what you will earn.

4) To "protect" you against low returns in the future, annuities offer a "guarantee." But it is a slippery guarantee. All it does is give you the right to withdraw your funds without a penalty if the return slips below a guaranteed level. That is important because the insurance company has the right to penalize you by as much as 25 percent for early withdrawals, meaning that the insurance company can legally keep a large chunk of your money. Unfortunately, the guaranteed return is very low. In other words, you could get stuck with a very low return and not be able to do anything with your money, unless you give a large portion of it to the insurer who issued the annuity.

Plus, if you buy an annuity instead of a zero-coupon Treasury bond when interest rates are high, you miss the chance to secure that high return for many years into the future. With zero-coupon bonds, your returns are locked in until maturity. The returns on annuities can fall to very low levels in the years ahead.

5) The interest you receive from annuities is dependent on the size of your investment. The $1,000 annuities pay the lowest rates. The yields on a $10,000 annuity are higher.

6) When the money is received, after you reach age 59 1/2, you pay taxes on it at your tax rate, which is why I am not sure annuities should be called "tax shelters."

Obviously, annuities are not my favorite investment when it comes to children.

Summary of our "investments du jour"

Individual stocks are a relatively risky choice for a child's portfolio. But if you believe that you know enough to beat the odds, you should consider buying stocks in your name. Later, you can transfer only the winners to your child's account before selling them. That way the profits will be taxed at your child's lower rate. And by keeping the losers in your name, you can use them as a tax deduction for yourself.

Mutual funds are probably the "safest" of the investments discussed in this chapter. But the risks are very real. And no matter how attractive the sales literature is, it is tough to argue that the" chance" of earning a little more than the yields on Treasury bonds is worth the risk.

One advantage, however, is that you can open an account at many mutual funds for as little as $250 and make additional investments of only $25.

And if you want to take the time to learn how to manage such an account, you can switch your investment from on type of fund to another with a phone call—from a growth fund, for example, to a bond fund, and then to a foreign stock fund, and so on.

Annuities, which only make sense if you or your spouse will be at least 59-1/2 years old when your child needs the earnings, have nothing to offer that is not achieved better with Series EE savings bonds. The only problem with Series EE savings bonds is that they sound dull.

Bonds that pay semi-annual dividends are not terrible. But they do not pay compound interest over time. Therefore, if you want to lock in high interest rates, zero-coupon Treasury bonds are a better choice. Plus, you can buy zero-coupon bonds for around $200. Regular bonds sell for about $1,000 each.

If you do decide to invest in regular bonds, be sure you know what you will do with the semiannual interest payments. One possibility is to invest the interest in Series EE savings bonds. Another is to use some of it to pay taxes on appreciating zero-coupon bonds.

Precious metals should be treated with caution. They do not pay interest. Prices can vary from dealer to dealer. And although they are viewed as protection against inflation, prices can stagnate or fall for years unless inflation soars to frightening levels. As a rule, these investments are better left to professionals. Also, after the inflation of the 1970's, it is virtually certain that market pressures will keep interest rates high enough to account for inflation, something that was not true in the 1960's and 1970's. Therefore, precious metals are no longer the only way to stay ahead of inflation.

Miscellaneous Ideas

This chapter is very personal—to me and, possibly, to you as well.

It is personal because it is part of real life—meaning that it is a look at the "non-financial" parts of child finance. It is about toys and antiques and the collections we loved as children.

I cannot possibly include every idea that could be a part of this chapter. I cannot even do justice to the few I will discuss.

But I could not write a book about saving and investing for children without including some thoughts on the things that touch our lives as children.

Antiques

When I was teaching economics in the SUNY system (a long time ago), I spent time looking for antique furniture. Not expensive antiques. Just nice old furniture.

I met an antique dealer who told me how he got started in the business.

When he was first married, he and his wife went out and bought a house full of new furniture. One year later, they had to move. And to make it as much fun as possible, they decided to sell everything and start fresh. They sold their furniture for 40- to 50-cents on the dollar, losing more than half the money they had spent just one year earlier.

He swore that he would never again buy a piece of new furniture. Little by little, they moved from used to old to antique. And one day he realized that they had collected so much stuff that he decided to open an antique store.

I never bought anything from him. But I did slowly accumulate a number of things that I liked. None were bought as investments. All were bought because I liked them. I still own some—pine blanket chest I bought at an auction in Vermont that is in my youngest daughter's room, some old pine chairs, and a pine table.

I also sold some things over the years. And I made a "profit" on each one.

My intention was not to make a profit. It was t buy what I liked, hoping that I would always be able to sell it for what I paid for it. Fortunately, what I liked was older furniture that appreciated, rather than depreciated, in value over the years.

You can do the same when furnishing your child's room—if you like antiques.

With a little time spent poking around antique stores, even household sales, you can find cribs, chests, rocking chairs, even quilts, that will hold their value. If you keep them long enough, they should gain in value.

You are not going to make a lot of money. But it can be fun. And if you keep the furniture, your child will almost certainly be able to sell it for a good price when he or she is an adult.

Baseball cards

I met someone in a coffee shop who told me that when he was eleven years old (in 1952) he collected baseball cards. He had a great time putting together a complete set of what is now a very valuable collector's item.

Of course, the cards were not worth anything in 1953. But he packed them away in a box, anyway, and put them in the attic.

About 25 years later, he found out that his long-forgotten baseball cards were worth at least $1,000.

So, the next time he went home to visit his parents, he dug around the attic looking for his "investment." But, he could not find his cards. And his parents had no idea what had happened to them.

Each year, the price of his old cards went up. And each summer that he returned home, he dug through the attic again.

As the years passed, his cards rose in value to about $100,000, because he had a number of single cards that were worth more than $10,000 each, by themselves.

Then, the cards were worth as much as $150,000. But they were still lost. His only consolation was that he probably would have sold the set for $1,000 if he had found it that first summer. His hope was that someday in the future, when the price is even higher, he would discover his lost treasure.

Today, collecting baseball cards can be serious business. Many investors buy new cards by the case and store the cases unopened. Each case contains 20 boxes of cards. But no one knows which cards. The contents of each case is a mystery.

No one knows exactly what is in each case. Because the cases are not opened. They are bought and sold according to the original year of issue. And their market value is a function of their "rookie cards"—how many rookies in a particular year went on to become stars! The more there were, the more that year's case is worth.

For example, there are new cases of baseball cards purchased for $230 that, a few years later, were worth between $5,400 and $6,000.

Whether or not the adult business of investing in baseball cards you never see sounds like fun, it has been a profitable venture. As far as I know, every case of cards has appreciated form its original price.

But there are even more investors and collectors who buy and sell individual cards or complete sets (52 cards).

For our purposes, however, the lesson is to take care of your child's collections. Aside from their sentimental value, they could someday be worth the down payment on a house or a large chunk of college costs.

Toys

Toys, unlike baseball cards or other kids' collectibles, are usually bought by parents, grandparents, or family friends.

But, wherever they come from, do not throw them away!

The collector demand for old toys has sent prices soaring. And "old" does not mean what "old" use to mean.

The toys of our youth are already valuable collectibles.

It used to be said that something had to be 100 years old before it could be called an antique. That may still be true. But antique or not, toys that are less than 30 years old are worth hundreds, sometimes thousands, of dollars.

Electric trains, Barbie dolls, comic books, whatever. Many are worth incredible sums today.

Which of today's toys will be worth the most in the future? There is no way of knowing for certain. So keep everything.

Art

In 1990, a Japanese businessman purchased a painting by Renoir for $82.5 million.

That is a little steep for decorating a child's room.

But it is not out of the question to buy real art for your child.

Posters and many original prints can be purchased for about the same price as department store "art." They are more beautiful. I believe they are more stimulating for children. And they might be sold for a profit sometime in the future.

Summary

The recommendation of this chapter is: Do not throw anything away.

But I do not want to turn something wonderful into a mercenary act.

Children's furniture, toys, collectibles, and art should be fun. They should help the child grow and develop. They should be a great pleasure. They should not be bought primarily as an investment.

But that does not mean you cannot have both.

If you are going to buy an electric train, call the local model railroad club. Ask about the best trains to buy. At worst, you will find out which trains are the highest quality. In any case, your child will enjoy having something of quality. And it might be worth a considerable sum of money in the future.

I think that we sometimes forget that children appreciate quality, even that they can tell the difference. But if you think back to when you were a child, you will remember how it felt to have something nice.

There is nothing wrong with putting in a little effort and a little thought when you buy something for your child. Or in taking care of it. And saving it.

The greatest benefit will most likely be the child's appreciation of quality.

"On the other hand, at current prices, that old set of baseball cards could now pay for four years of tuition at a private college or university.

A handbook

This is a handbook, not an encyclopedia.

As such, it should do more than simply list all the possibilities.

A handbook should offer guidance, not just information.

If you need bits and pieces of information on all sorts of investment ideas, the bookstores and libraries are full of 600- to 800-page investment "encyclopedias."

The purpose of this book is to fill another need—the need to be able to do something with all that information.

If there is a model for our handbook, it would be a "how to sail" book. There are many books that tell you all sorts of things about all sorts of sailboats. But when it gets down to you and your boat, you need more than an encyclopedia listing all the boats ever made. You need more than an explanation of the advantages and disadvantages of each boat. You need to know more than where to find all the great places in the world to sail. If you want to learn to sail your boat, you need a book that tells you "how to sail!"

And if you want to save and invest for your children's future, this book is an attempt to tell you how to do it.

There is another important similarity between this handbook and a handbook on sailing.

When you sail, you have to work within the constraints of the physical environment.

Financial plans are the same. They always exist within an overall environment that exists and within the limitations of your own financial situation.

It might be fun to talk about how things used to be. About what you would do if things were different. About how much money can be made in the stock market if you pick the right stock at the right time. About what you would do if interest rates went above 20 percent again (which they did just before the Carter-Reagan election). About what you would do if inflation soared back into double-digits. Or about how bad the tax laws are.

But if you are on a small boat, caught in a storm, it will not do much good to think about what you would do if you had a bigger boat or a safer boat, or what you would do if there were no storm. If you are going to make it through and enjoy the years ahead, your job is to do the best you can with what you have.

This book offers the best advice I can give you on what to do for your child's financial future, (or your grandchild's).

I have three final recommendations, or suggestions.

1) Do not make long-term goal setting your first step. Let your first step be our shoebox. Then get a Social Security number for your child. Then open a Coverdell account. Then buy a few zero-coupon Treasury bonds through the Coverdell account. Then, after a year or so, sit down and see how much you have accomplished.

Very simply, get started before you set any long-term goals.

2) Next, set realistic goals. You can always raise your goals. But if you have to miss a few months, or a year, forget it. As soon as you can, pick up where you left off. You can try to make up for what you had to skip. But that should not be a major goal. It is much better to have a slightly smaller future portfolio than to abandon your entire plan because of a temporary setback.

Whatever you do is great. So concentrate on doing something instead of on what you might not be able to do because of circumstances you cannot control.

College scholarships

When your child is getting ready for college, check to see if he or she might qualify for scholarships. But many of those scholarships are so narrowly defined that it is almost impossible to qualify.

In any case, scholarships come later. So you should not count on them as anything other than a possibility.

However, if you approach scholarship applications like a real job, your chances of success will improve considerably.

Prepaid college

Prepaying college tuition is a relatively new idea. And it can be done using a 529 Prepaid College Plan.

If such a plan seems to make sense for you and your children, check it out carefully. Is there a refund if your child decides on another school or a college in another state? What if your child decides not to go to college at all? What about entrance requirements?

Plus: Tuition is only one part of total college costs. So do not forget about saving for the rest.

If the prepayment is for four years of tuition, do not forget that many students take six years or more to get a "four year" degree. So you may need to cover another two or more years.

Do you have to make a single payment or is there a scheduled payment plan? In either case, compare it with other alternatives.

The point is, if you prepay tuition years ahead of time, the college or state is going to invest your money. And you should think about what you can earn if you invest the money in a Coverdell ESA, a 529 plan, and/or a Roth IRA.

Conclusion

I want to conclude by reminding you of the three principles of successful investing:

1) Keep it simple.
2) Relax.
3) Maintain control.

Do not get carried away with your plans or your goals. Just do what you can. When new ideas come along, compare them with the investments you are already making. But that means you had better be doing something. The ideas in this book give you something you can do, beginning today.

Many years ago, in one of his most quoted poems, Robert Frost wrote the lines:

The woods are lovely, dark, and deep,
But I have promises to keep,
And miles to go before I sleep,
And miles to go before I sleep.

The world is exciting. But we only get one ride. So give your children a chance to have the best possible journey.

About the Author

Dr. Dennis Paulaha received a B.S. in Business Administration from the University of Minnesota, an M.A. in Economics from the University of Minnesota, and a Ph.D. in Economics from the University of Washington.

As an academic economist, he taught undergraduate and graduate macroeconomic and microeconomic theory, monetary theory and policy, environmental economics, and special issues courses.

He has written on economic and financial issues for the public.

And he was Staff Economist for one of America's largest precious metals firms, and Vice President of Marketing for a brokerage company with national sales.

Notes

You can use this, and the following pages, to make notes on books, articles, radio, and TV shows, etc. that add to your knowledge or have ideas you want to remember. You can also write down numbers you want to keep.

NOTES